ideals

THANKSGIVING

D1254556

Dear Lord, my thanks I offer Thee
For priceless gifts bestowed in me!
I use them constantly, and yet
The *Giver* I sometimes forget!
Thanks for my *eyes*, dear Lord—I see
The glories that encircle me.
While through my *ears* come speech and songs—
The world of sound to me belongs!
My *hands*, with their swift sense of touch,
Are daily blessings—means so much!
My *voice*, too, is a gift from God—
A constant help along life's road.
My *mind*, my *heart*, my *soul*—all three
Are precious treasures, Lord, from Thee.
For *life* on this Thanksgiving Day,
Accept my gratitude, I pray!

Dr. W. J. Thompson

Publisher, James A. Kuse
Managing Editor, Ralph Luedtke
Editor/Ideals, Colleen Callahan Gonring
Associate Editor, Linda Robinson
Production Manager, Mark Brunner
Photographic Editor, Gerald Koser
Copy Editor, Norma Barnes
Art Editor, Duane Weaver
Contributing Editor, Beverly Wiersum Charette

ISBN 0-89542-335-9 295

IDEALS—Vol. 37, No. 7 October MCMLXXX. IDEALS (ISSN 0019-137X) is published eight times a year,
January, February, April, June, July, September, October, November
by IDEALS PUBLISHING CORPORATION, 11315 Watertown Plank Road, Milwaukee, Wis. 53226
Second class postage paid at Milwaukee, Wisconsin. Copyright © MCMLXXX by IDEALS PUBLISHING CORPORATION.
All rights reserved. Title IDEALS registered U.S. Patent Office.
Published Simultaneously in Canada.

ONE YEAR SUBSCRIPTION—eight consecutive issues as published—$15.95
TWO YEAR SUBSCRIPTION—sixteen consecutive issues as published—$27.95
SINGLE ISSUES—$2.95

The cover and entire contents of IDEALS are fully protected by copyright and must
not be reproduced in any manner whatsoever. Printed and bound in U.S.A.

An Autumn Wood

The mellow fragrance of an autumn wood
Flows like a gossamer veil above the bed
Of leaves and mosses. . .Here a dulcet mood
Haloed in gold, transforms the motley spread,
The wild rose petals and the minty spears
Of sundry plants exude a spicy blend. . .
A honeyed breeze cavorts as evening nears,
And everything bespeaks a rural trend.

A fragile deer stands motionless beside
A placid pool, wrapt in pervading peace. . .
A forest vastness, where small creatures hide,
Until the sounds of human movements cease.

An autumn wood will hold you in its spell,
And sagas of the centuries will tell.

Ella Castle Nedrow

Corn Is King!

Beverly Wiersum Charette

What do Lawrence Welk, Andy Williams, Skitch Henderson and John Philip Sousa all have in common? They have all played the Palace—the Corn Palace in Mitchell, South Dakota.

Every year since 1902, Mitchellites have booked top name entertainment to appear during their week-long harvest festival held late in September in their world-famous, and world's only, Corn Palace.

There is no doubt that these celebrities never fail to attract record-breaking crowds, but the biggest attraction is still the Palace itself.

What is a Corn Palace? Curiously enough, a Corn Palace is just what its name implies—a palace made of corn. Technically, it is constructed of brick; but over all, on both the exterior and interior, it displays designs and large murals created entirely out of corn and other grains and grasses native to South Dakota. Each year the Palace is completely stripped and redecorated with designs indicative of a brand new theme. Although turrets and Moorish minarets

and kiosks contribute an eastern flavor, the total effect of the Corn Palace is distinctly western, from its architectural design to the scenes depicted in its murals. In all its uniqueness the Corn Palace represents the imagination, ingenuity and energy of a pragmatic yet creative people.

For twenty-five years the Corn Palace directly represented the talents of South Dakota's Artist Laureate, Oscar Howe. From 1948 through 1971, this already distinguished artist, a native of the state, designed and directed the execution of the giant panels. For this full-blooded Yanktonaise Sioux, who rose above a childhood of poverty and prejudice, the murals became an outward expression of emotion for his people and their culture.

Although demands on Howe's time no longer allow him to continue working on the Palace, today he looks back on those years of designing "with nostalgia and a deep sense of pride." Howe and his predecessors and successors have good reason to feel proud. Working with decorations restricted to the grains and grasses of the state, they and their crews have achieved tremendous results.

From the beginning, the whole process of decorating depends a great deal on the farmers. Once the artist has developed a scheme of design based on that year's particular theme, he gives his corn, grain and grass requirements to those farmers who specialize in growing produce exclusively for the Palace. Meanwhile, the artist designs and paints each panel separately in miniature, later scaling it to full size on black roofing paper. This paper, in turn, is tacked to the panel on the building as a guide for placement of the ears according to direction and color—white, red, blue, or varying shades of yellow. After the trim surrounding the panels is nailed in place, the ears of corn are cut in half lengthwise by a power saw and nailed flat side to the panel. The crews work from scaffolds, finishing one panel at a time until the Corn Palace has been completely redone, usually two or three days prior to the festival to ensure the freshest and most colorful appearance. Mitchellites have refined this creative

process to a science, a science that has resulted from nearly a century of practice.

Back in 1892, two enterprising businessmen borrowed the idea of a grain palace from two neighboring communities that had experimented unsuccessfully with the concept. L.O. Gale and Louis E. Beckwith held the opinion that Mitchell's city residents and rural neighbors deserved a special place set aside for a grand harvest celebration. The first Corn Belt Exposition, as Mitchell's early Corn Palace Festivals were called, achieved such immediate success that a second one was held the following year. Plagued by drought, depression and financial difficulties, the third did not occur until 1900 and the fourth not until 1902, when it played an integral part in Mitchell's unsuccessful bid for the location of the state capital. By 1905, however, the event was so popular that Mitchellites built a replacement with a much larger crowd capacity and renamed it the Corn Palace.

Three Corn Palaces later, the cosmetics have varied a great deal from the original. The second wooden frame building has also been razed and replaced by one that is more structurally sound and permanent. The original geometric designs long ago gave way to pictures and scenes that have evolved from educational to patriotic to entertaining to ecological subject matter. The early 1940s represent the only departure from the traditional grain ornamentation; at that time city leaders agreed to suspend the use of produce as decoration for the duration of the war, and substituted paintings for corncob panels.

Today the present structure functions not only as the highlight of the harvest celebration, but also as a civic center utilized for conventions, public meetings, music festivals, dances and college and high school basketball games.

One question concerning the Corn Palace remains unanswered. Where there is a palace, is there a sovereign? After all this time the answer should be obvious: in Mitchell, South Dakota, corn reigns supreme!

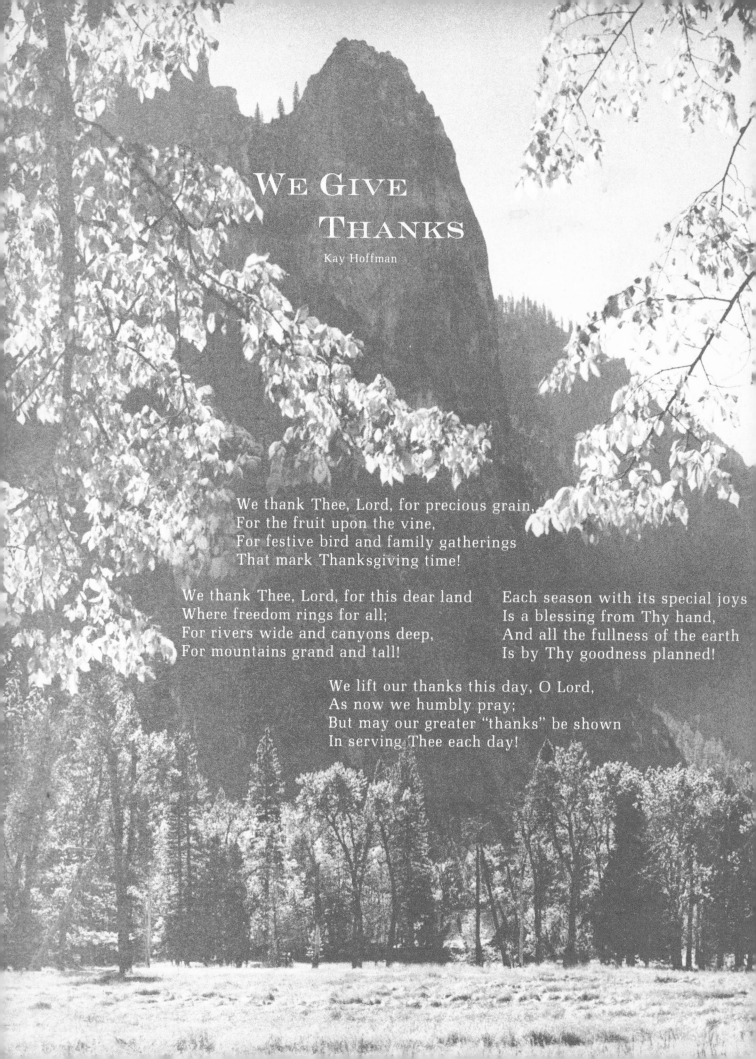

WE GIVE
THANKS

Kay Hoffman

We thank Thee, Lord, for precious grain,
For the fruit upon the vine,
For festive bird and family gatherings
That mark Thanksgiving time!

We thank Thee, Lord, for this dear land
Where freedom rings for all;
For rivers wide and canyons deep,
For mountains grand and tall!

Each season with its special joys
Is a blessing from Thy hand,
And all the fullness of the earth
Is by Thy goodness planned!

We lift our thanks this day, O Lord,
As now we humbly pray;
But may our greater "thanks" be shown
In serving Thee each day!

A Forest Hymn

William Cullen Bryant

The groves were God's first temples. Ere man learned
To hew the shaft, and lay the architrave,
And spread the roof above them—ere he framed
The lofty vault, to gather and roll back
The sound of anthems; in the darkling wood,
Amid the cool and silence, he knelt down,
And offered to the Mightiest solemn thanks
And supplications, for his simple heart
Might not resist the sacred influences
Which, from the stilly twilight of the place,
And from the gray old trunks that high in heaven
Mingled their mossy boughs, and from the sound
Of the invisible breath that swayed at once
All their green tops, stole over him, and bowed
His spirit with the thought of boundless power
And inaccessible majesty. Ah, why
Should we, in the world's riper years, neglect
God's ancient sanctuaries, and adore
Only among the crowd, and under roofs
That our frail hands have raised? Let me, at least,
Here, in the shadow of this aged wood,
Offer one hymn—thrice happy, if it find
Acceptance in His ear.

Father, thy hand
Hath reared these venerable columns, thou
Didst weave this verdant roof. Thou didst look down
Upon the naked earth, and, forthwith, rose
All these fair ranks of trees. They, in thy sun,
Budded, and shook their green leaves in thy breeze,
And shot toward heaven. The century-living crow
Whose birth was in their tops, grew old and died
Among their branches, till, at last, they stood,
As now they stand, massy, and tall, and dark,
Fit shrine for humble worshipper to hold
Communion with his Maker. These dim vaults,
These winding aisles, of human pomp or pride
Report not. No fantastic carvings show
The boast of our vain race to change the form
Of thy fair works. But thou art here—thou fill'st
The solitude. Thou art in the soft winds
That run along the summit of these trees
In music; thou art in the cooler breath
That from the inmost darkness of the place
Comes, scarcely felt; the barky trunks, the ground,
The fresh moist ground, are all instinct with thee.

Here is continual worship; Nature, here,
In the tranquillity that thou dost love,
Enjoys thy presence. Noiselessly, around,
From perch to perch, the solitary bird
Passes; and yon clear spring, that, midst its herbs
Wells softly forth and wandering steeps the roots
Of half the mighty forest, tells no tale
Of all the good it does. Thou hast not left
Thyself without a witness, in the shades,
Of thy perfections. Grandeur, strength, and grace
Are here to speak of thee. This mighty oak—
By whose immovable stem I stand and seem
Almost annihilated—not a prince,
In all that proud, old world beyond the deep,
E'er wore his crown as loftily as he.
Wears the green coronal of leaves with which
Thy hand has graced him. Nestled at his root
Is beauty, such as blooms not in the glare
Of the broad sun. That delicate forest flower,
With scented breath and look so like a smile,
Seems, as it issues from the shapeless mould,
An emanation of the indwelling Life,
A visible token of the upholding Love,
That are the soul of this great universe.

My heart is awed within me when I think
Of the great miracle that still goes on,
In silence, round me—the perpetual work
Of thy creation, finished, yet renewed
Forever. Written on thy works I read
The lesson of thy own eternity.
Lo! All grow old and die—but see again,
How on the faltering footsteps of decay
Youth presses,—ever gay and beautiful youth
In all its beautiful forms. These lofty trees
Wave not less proudly that their ancestors
Moulder beneath them. Oh, there is not lost
One of earth's charms: upon her bosom yet,
After the flight of untold centuries,
The freshness of her far beginning lies
And yet shall lie. Life mocks the idle hate
Of his arch-enemy Death—yea, seats himself
Upon the tyrant's throne—the sepulchre,
And of the triumphs of his ghastly foe
Makes his own nourishment, for he came forth
From thine own bosom, and shall have no end.

There have been holy men who hid themselves
Deep in the woody wilderness, and gave
Their lives to thought and prayer, till they outlived
The generation born with them, nor seemed
Less aged than the hoary trees and rocks
Around them; and there have been holy men
Who deemed it were not well to pass life thus.

But let me often to these solitudes
Retire, and in thy presence reassure
My feeble virtue. Here its enemies,
The passions, at thy plainer footsteps shrink
And tremble and are still. O God! When thou
Dost scare the world with tempest, set on fire
The heavens with falling thunderbolts, or fill,
With all the waters of the firmament,
The swift dark whirlwind that uproots the woods
And drowns the villages; when, at thy call,
Uprises the great deep and throws himself
Upon the continent, and overwhelms
Its cities—who forgets not, at the sight
Of these tremendous tokens of thy power,
His pride, and lays his strifes and follies by?

Oh, from these sterner aspects of thy face
Spare me and mine, nor let us need the wrath
Of the mad unchained elements to teach
Who rules them. Be it ours to meditate,
In these calm shades, thy milder majesty,
And to the beautiful order of thy works
Learn to conform the order of our lives.

Autumn Blessings

Alice Leedy Mason

Peace spreads through the valley,
  Geese sail overhead,
Apples in the orchard
  Are clustered gold and red.

Stone walls fence the farm lands,
  Sheaves stand proud and tall,
Tip-to-toe the mountain
  Is wearing shades of fall.

Vesper bells ring softly,
  Almost like a prayer.
Leaves rain gold and scarlet—
  They flutter in the air.

Brooks send leafy vessels
  Onward to the seas.
Village roads keep winding
  Through avenues of trees.

The little church bids welcome,
  Dressed in rosy vines.
High above its steeple
  The moon of harvest shines.

God's Corner
Gertrude M. Puelicher

October is a delightful month in the north woods. The nights are cold, the days warm and sunny. My boardwalk through the black spruce forest urges me to take advantage of each day because before long that particular trail will be off-bounds—snow-covered trails are more conducive to snow-shoeing or skiing than walking.

Three deer are in the meadow. They smell Jacques before he sees them, and off they go with the graceful leaps and bounds of ballet dancers. A hawk skims high over the treetops, clearly defined against the blue sky. Ordinarily I don't think kindly of hawks; they destroy the small woods animals. Today, however, even the hawk fits into the mellow warmth of the sun and of my mood.

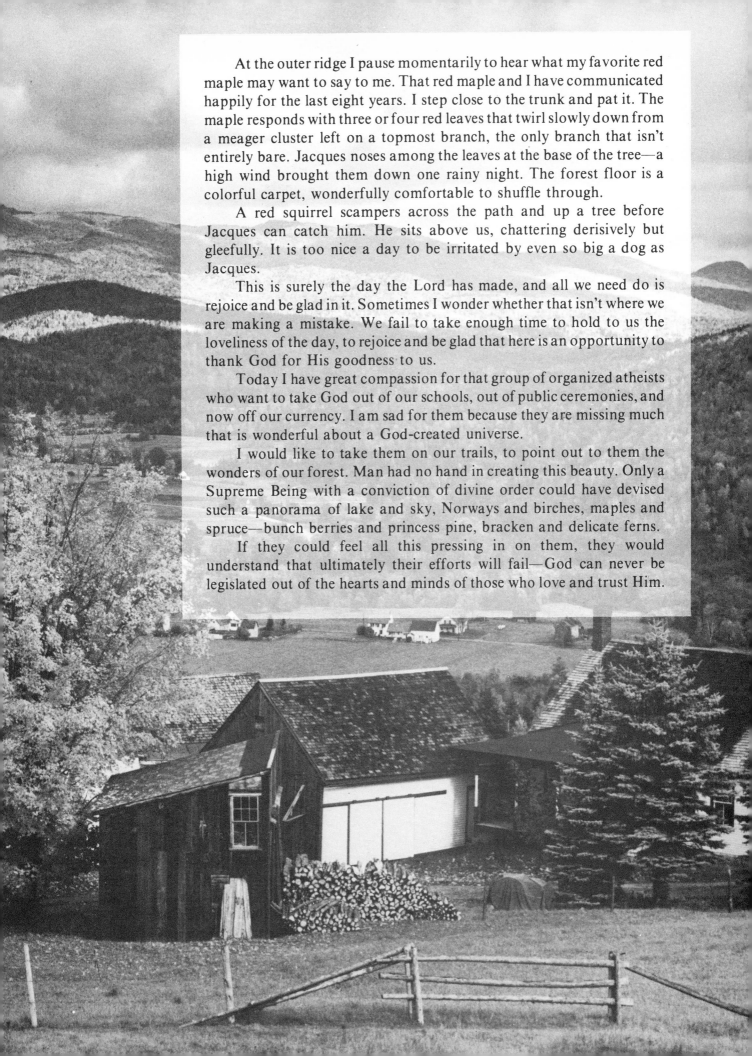

At the outer ridge I pause momentarily to hear what my favorite red maple may want to say to me. That red maple and I have communicated happily for the last eight years. I step close to the trunk and pat it. The maple responds with three or four red leaves that twirl slowly down from a meager cluster left on a topmost branch, the only branch that isn't entirely bare. Jacques noses among the leaves at the base of the tree—a high wind brought them down one rainy night. The forest floor is a colorful carpet, wonderfully comfortable to shuffle through.

A red squirrel scampers across the path and up a tree before Jacques can catch him. He sits above us, chattering derisively but gleefully. It is too nice a day to be irritated by even so big a dog as Jacques.

This is surely the day the Lord has made, and all we need do is rejoice and be glad in it. Sometimes I wonder whether that isn't where we are making a mistake. We fail to take enough time to hold to us the loveliness of the day, to rejoice and be glad that here is an opportunity to thank God for His goodness to us.

Today I have great compassion for that group of organized atheists who want to take God out of our schools, out of public ceremonies, and now off our currency. I am sad for them because they are missing much that is wonderful about a God-created universe.

I would like to take them on our trails, to point out to them the wonders of our forest. Man had no hand in creating this beauty. Only a Supreme Being with a conviction of divine order could have devised such a panorama of lake and sky, Norways and birches, maples and spruce—bunch berries and princess pine, bracken and delicate ferns.

If they could feel all this pressing in on them, they would understand that ultimately their efforts will fail—God can never be legislated out of the hearts and minds of those who love and trust Him.

For a Child

Fanny Stearns Davis

Your friends shall be the Tall Wind,
  The River and the Tree,
The Sun that laughs and marches,
  The Swallows and the Sea.

Your prayers shall be the murmur
  Of grasses in the rain,
The song of wildwood thrushes
  That makes God glad again.

And you shall run and wander,
  And you shall dream and sing
Of brave things and bright things
  Beyond the swallow's wings.

And you shall envy no man,
  Nor hurt your heart with sighs,
For I will keep you simple
  That God may make you wise.

Playful Autumn

Michele Arrieh

Autumn is a playful child,
  A lively little girl
With eyes the blue of azure skies
  And bouncing golden curls.

Playing mischief merrily,
  A paintbrush in her hand,
She changes lush green scenery
  To an amber, scarlet land.

No one stops her as she romps
  Through countryside and town.
She runs so fast that in her path
  The leaves come swirling down.

Father Winter sends a message
  That she must obey,
"It's time to come in from your frolic
  And to end your play."

The Apple—
Nature's Gift to Man
Michele Arrieh

Tasty and nutritious and readily available all year long, the apple is commonly taken for granted. This juicy, sweet fruit, eaten in a variety of ways, has been a source of food for man throughout the ages. Scholars surmise that apples may have originated in southwest Asia where, coincidentally, the Bible places the Garden of Eden. It is a known fact, however, that apples were used by primitive man long before recorded history. Archaeologists have found carbonized remains of apples in prehistoric lake dwellings in Switzerland dating back to the Iron Age. There is also evidence that apples were eaten and preserved by slicing and sun-drying as far back as the Stone Age in Europe.

Information about apples can be found in some of man's earliest recordings. The ancient annals of Babylon, Egypt, and China reveal that man understood, as many as twenty centuries ago, that apples do not reproduce true from seed but must be bud grafted in order to maintain a particular variety. Invading Roman legions under Caesar introduced apples to the British Isles, where they have flourished ever since. In time, apples were planted throughout Europe.

The first settlers in this country found that the apples they knew were not indigenous to their new homeland. The closest substitute was a sour crab apple, which was of limited use for food and not cultivated by the Indians. So fond were they of the apple, however, that the settlers sought ways to provide their families and themselves with this favorite fruit. Governor Endicott of the Massachusetts Bay Colony is credited with growing the first apple tree in this country from a seedling brought from Europe. The first apple crops in the New World were harvested by the Pilgrims in Massachusetts and the colonists in Jamestown, Virginia. Even George Washington and Thomas Jefferson, both diligent students of horticulture, planted and maintained beautiful apple orchards on their estates.

As the early settlers traveled west in covered wagons, they carried, as treasured and carefully protected cargo, apple trees and "scion wood" for grafting. Apples were also carried by Indians, traders and missionaries into the new frontier.

In the early 1800s, a man by the name of Jonathan Chapman gained a wide reputation for his travels through the territories of Ohio, Indiana, and Illinois, preaching his Swedenborgian faith and planting apple trees wherever he went. He lived frugally, never owned a home, dressed in meager clothes and often went barefoot in summer and winter. Upon his head he wore a tin pan, which served the dual purpose of hat and stew pan for cooking his food. With a pocketful of apple seeds, he traveled throughout most of the Ohio Valley, working his way west. As he went along, he planted and tended seedling apple tree nurseries for the early frontier settlers. Thus, the legend of "Johnny Appleseed" was born. A peace-loving man, Johnny Appleseed was also a friend to the Indians and sought no harm to any living creature. He became known for his courage and dedication to his fellowman as well as for the thousands of apple trees he planted. Today, his life and work are commemorated in a park and memorial in Fort Wayne, Indiana, where he died in 1845.

Throughout antiquity the apple has been used symbolically. The Book of Genesis

continued

describes a certain tree bearing fruit in the Garden of Eden to which God forbade access to Adam and Eve. Although the "forbidden fruit" is never directly named in the Bible, the implicit assumption has always been that it was an apple that led to man's downfall. The "knowledge" inherent in the tree and its fruit is taken to mean the ability to distinguish between good and evil.

The Lord Jehovah's great regard for the Israelites is implied several times in the Old Testament by the expression, "the apple of his eye." "For he that touches you toucheth the apple of His eye," Moses warns in Deuteronomy. Jeremiah alludes, in Lamentations, to the more commonly understood use of the phrase when he says, "... let the tears run down like a river day and night; give thyself no rest; let not the apple of thine eye cease." This statement links the pupil of the eye with its likeness, the apple, a solid sphere, meaning that the Israelites were as precious to God as the pupils of man's eyes are to him.

In classical mythology, the apple is often made of gold, clear measure of the esteem in which it was held. One story tells of a beauty contest between the goddesses, Hera, Athena and Aphrodite, which the mortal Paris is chosen to judge. Aphrodite bribes Paris, offering him the most beautiful mortal woman for his wife if he will grant her the golden apple inscribed, "to the fairest." Paris accepts the offer—though his bride is to be Helen, who is already married to Menelaus—thus igniting the long and tragic Trojan War. In both Greek and Roman mythology the apple was often a symbol of love and beauty.

Another story describes a wonderful tree which grows in the Garden of the Gods, having sprung up on the day that Zeus and Hera were wed in that garden. This magnificent tree bears golden apples with a "taste of honey" and the ability to cure all illnesses.

Ages later in Devonshire, England, the saying arose: "Ate an apfel avore gwain to bed. Makes the doctor beg his bread." Today we claim that "An apple a day keeps the doctor away." There is more truth in that saying than might be expected, since recent studies show that apples contain certain substances that aid in the body's digestion and regulatory systems, help fight body toxins and control the levels of cholesterol in the blood. Studies have also shown that the eating of apples results in a marked reduction in dental decay because apples act as their own toothbrush.

The apple is also the focal point of many stories which have grown up around actual characters. Sir Isaac Newton is said to have "discovered" the law of gravity while sitting under an apple tree. Supposedly, by watching the simple action of apples falling to the ground, Newton was able to make his insightful observations. Legend also has it that William Tell shot an apple off his son's head at the order of Austrian invaders of Switzerland.

In today's storehouse of phrases and expressions, the apple still has a prominent place. "Mother, apple pie, and baseball" is a phrase which connotes wholesomeness and all-American standards. "Apple polisher" or "apple shiner" became an expression in this country in the 1920s and refers to a flatterer or one who is trying to impress another, deriving its meaning from the older tradition of the eager student who gives his teacher an apple. The expression, "apple knocker," for a rustic type, has come into use in this century, as has the term "Big Apple," meaning New York City.

It may be surprising to discover that the ordinary little apple is quite a famous and historically illustrious fruit. Man has known for a long time that the apple is one of nature's miracles—a colorful and delicious "package" of health-giving nutrients and eating enjoyment. Maybe Eve was tempted by an apple, but it has been a blessing to mankind ever since!

An Apple a Day
In a Tasty Way

APPLE CRISP

6 apples
1 c. flour
½ c. butter
½ c. brown sugar
2 T. sugar
½ t. cinnamon

Peel, core and slice apples. Place in a buttered 8″ x 12″ pan. Mix together flour, sugars, butter and cinnamon until crumbly. Sprinkle over apples. Bake at 350° for 30 minutes. Serve warm, topped with whipped cream, ice cream or milk.

BAKED APPLE MERINGUES

3 egg whites
⅜ t. salt
½ t. almond extract
½ c. sugar
   Almonds, slivered
6 apples, baked and cooled

Place egg whites in a bowl and add salt and extract; beat until stiff. Gradually add sugar, beating until smooth and glossy. Place apples on a cookie sheet. Cover each apple with a thick coating of meringue. Sprinkle with a few slivered almonds and bake at 325° for 15 minutes, or until light brown. Can be served as a dessert or as part of the meal.

APPLE DESSERT CRUNCH

1 c. quick-cooking oats
1 c. brown sugar
⅔ c. flour
⅓ c. butter
4 c. diced apples
1 t. cinnamon
1 c. sugar

Mix together the oats, brown sugar, flour, and butter. Combine apples, cinnamon, and sugar. Arrange in a well-buttered 8″ x 11″ pan. Sprinkle over the apple mixture. Bake at 350° for about 30 minutes. Serve warm, topped with whipped cream or ice cream.

DUTCH APPLE KUCHEN

¾ c. flour
1 T. sugar
¼ t. baking powder
6 T. butter
¼ t. salt
½ c. chopped almonds
3 egg yolks
1 c. sugar
1 c. sour cream
6 apples, peeled, cored and chopped

Mix together the flour, sugar, baking powder, butter and salt. Pat mixture into a buttered 7″ x 11″ pie plate. Set aside. Mix together almonds, egg yolks, sugar and sour cream, blending well. Stir in apples. Pour apple mixture onto the unbaked crust. Bake at 350° for 30 minutes.

APPLE STRUDEL

½ c. butter
2 c. flour
1 t. salt
1 t. sugar
½ t. baking powder
½ c. sour cream
¼ c. melted butter
1½ t. cinnamon
½ c. sugar
4 apples, finely chopped
1 egg yolk mixed with 1 t. water

Cut butter into flour, salt, sugar and baking powder. Stir in sour cream, mixing thoroughly. Divide dough into four equal portions. Roll each portion into an 8″ x 10″ rectangle. Spread with melted butter. Combine cinnamon and sugar. Divide chopped apple among rectangles, then sprinkle with sugar and cinnamon mixture. Roll up as for a jelly roll. Place on a buttered cookie sheet. Brush tops of strudels with the egg yolk-water mixture. Sprinkle additional cinnamon-sugar on top. Bake at 400° for 10 minutes. Reduce heat to 350° and bake 25 minutes longer. Drizzle Thin Icing over strudels. Makes 4 strudels.

THIN ICING

1½ c. confectioners' sugar
1 t. almond extract
1½ T. milk or water

Combine all ingredients, stirring until smooth.

Thanksgiving

No warm greeting was in store
As they stepped on a bleak and wintry shore,
No shelter from the freezing gale,
Then one last goodbye as their ship set sail.

But courage sustained them in their flight
With love of God and belief in right.
It saw them through a great ordeal,
And nothing stopped their devoted zeal.

They built log homes; their church arose,
A place to worship as they chose.
They hunted in the forest near
For wild turkeys and for deer.

The Indians taught them how to grow
The corn that flourished, row on row,
And how to tap the maple tree
So sap could flow out, clean and free.

So let us bow our heads this day,
As a prayer of gratitude we say
For those brave Pilgrims' first Thanksgivi
And for this dear land in which we're livir

Eleanor Ell

The Landing
of the Pilgrim Fathers

The breaking waves dashed high
On a stern and rock-bound coast,
And the woods against a stormy sky
Their giant branches tossed,
And the heavy night hung dark
The hills and waters o'er,
When a band of exiles moored their bark
On the wild New England shore.
Not as the conqueror comes,
They, the true-hearted came;
Not with the roll of stirring drums
And the trumpet that sings of fame;
Not as the flying come
In silence and in fear,
They shook the depths of the desert gloom
With their hymns of lofty cheer.

Amidst the storm they sang,
And the stars heard, and the sea;
And the sounding aisles of the dim woods rang
To the anthem of the free.
The ocean eagle soared
From his nest by the white wave's foam,
And the rocking pines of the forest roared;
This was their welcome home.

There were men with hoary hair
Amidst that pilgrim band;
Why had they come to wither there,
Away from their childhood's land?
There was woman's fearless eye,
Lit by her deep love's truth;
There was manhood's brow serenely high,
And the fiery heart of youth.

What sought they thus afar?
Bright jewels of the mine?
The wealth of seas, the spoils of war?
They sought a faith's pure shrine.
Ay, call it holy ground,
The soil where first they trod,
They have left unstained what there they found,
Freedom to worship God.

Felicia D. Hemans

Autumn Moments

As I looked o'er the garden this morning,
The sun came pouring down
And capped the autumn landscape
With a shimmering golden crown.

Dew from the cool of evening
Was clinging to every blade,
While the robin on the tree branch
Sang his farewell serenade.

Too soon it will be over.
These precious days of fall
And all this crimson splendor
Will bow to winter's call.

But just for now I marvel
At the beauty everywhere
And thank the Lord who lets us
These autumn moments share.

Shirley Sallay

The First Yankees

Edith Butler

"God sifted a whole nation that He might send choice grain into the wilderness." These words were spoken by a sturdy old Puritan in 1688, for the courageous men and women who were to be the founders of New England were not mere adventurers. They were not poor people coming to a new country for economic reasons. They came from comfortable homes; indeed, some were wealthy and most were well educated. But so great was their desire to find a land where they would be free to follow their faith and religious convictions that on September 16, 1620, one hundred and two Pilgrims set sail for America in the *Mayflower*. Crowded and ill, they were tossed about on the wild and stormy Atlantic for over two months.

After a fearful trip and having been driven far off their course, they landed, on the twenty-first of November, 1620, at Cape Cod. They dropped anchor in the harbor of what was to be Province-town, and, in the cabin of the battered *Mayflower*, they framed the document which was to be the foundation of American liberty, the memorable Mayflower Compact. Written and signed by the Pilgrim fathers, this compact provided for a civic body to make laws by which they were to be governed in fairness and justice to every member. They also agreed to abide by these laws for the common good of all.

It was a cruelly bitter season of the year to be undertaking the exploration and settling of a new world. These people faced unknown hardship and dangers. Five weeks of valuable time were consumed in seeking out the best possible location for the town which they hoped to establish. Led by Captain Miles Standish, a party of sixteen men explored the coastline in the tiny open shallop from the *Mayflower*. While walking along the shore one day, they saw five or six Indians who, on seeing them, disappeared into the woods. Further on, they found land that showed signs of having been under cultivation. They dug down into a heap of sand and to their great joy found a basket of Indian corn. It was reassuring also to find plenty of game, for there was an abundance of partridge, geese, ducks and deer. Once they were attacked by a small party of Indians, but these were driven off without loss of life among the Pilgrims.

After many days of searching they found themselves in the harbor of what was to be Plymouth. The small exploring party had suffered terribly from exposure to cold and snow and wet, frozen clothes in a climate more rigorous than they had ever known. On landing, they found evidence of cornfields, good drinking water, and the location for which they had been looking so long. Here, too, the harbor seemed desirable for the shipping which they hoped to develop. Bearing this welcome news, the weary men returned to the *Mayflower*, and so at last that valiant ship sailed into Plymouth harbor.

In spite of the storms and cold of winter, the men began building their homes in the spot which had been chosen and named Plymouth. It was fortunate for the Pilgrims that the Indians did not bother them that winter, though the smoke from their campfires was sometimes seen at a distance. Other enemies, however, had taken their toll, and by spring nearly half of the little colony had died from hardship, illness and privation. Nevertheless they would not return when the *Mayflower* set sail for England in April. For as William Brewster said, "It is not with us as with men whom small things can discourage or small discontentments cause to wish themselves at home again."

The work of building homes for the young colony went on. By the end of the summer that followed the men had built seven houses and a fort at the top of the hill and had cleared approximately twenty-five acres of land.

During the late winter the Pilgrims had been successful in establishing friendly relations with the Indians. In March, 1621, a treaty had been made between them and Massasoit, the great sachem of the Wampanoag, the Massachusetts Indians. Both parties agreed to keep the peace and to refrain from infringing on the rights of each other. Any offenders on either side were to be duly punished. This treaty also provided for mutual assistance in the event of an attack by the enemies of either

party. This is the oldest diplomatic record in the history of New England. It was drawn up in a single day, the pipe of peace was smoked, and the treaty was kept faithfully for more than half a century.

The Pilgrims had raised money for their venture to America by borrowing from wealthy Englishmen, and, in return, they were under obligation to search for exports to send back to England, such as furs, fish and choice wood. Twenty-one years after they had landed at Plymouth they were free from this debt and possessed all rights to the lands for which they had worked so hard and suffered so much.

During the spring and summer of 1621 the friendly Indians had instructed the Pilgrims in the cultivation of their corn. Without this help, the infant colony might not have survived the second winter at Plymouth. They had brought no cattle, horses or sheep with them from England, and their garden seeds did not thrive in the sandy soil of Plymouth. It was well that they had planted twenty of their cleared acres in Indian corn or they would have had little to harvest, for their barley was "indifferent good" and their peas burned and dried up so that they were not worth gathering.

When autumn came the corn harvest was good and fish and game were plentiful; so the Pilgrims decided to hold a feast of gratitude to the Almighty God who had spared their lives and provided them with sustenance. Four men were sent on a hunting expedition to bring back enough game for a three-day feast, and they invited Massasoit and ninety of his people to this first Thanksgiving dinner. The Indians brought five deer, their contribution to the festivities.

In 1630, inspired by favorable reports from this pioneer settlement, great numbers of Puritans began to come to this country to establish new settlements all along the coast of New England. These young colonies endured every kind of hardship, but their faith gave them the courage and energy to lay the foundations for a country which today enjoys so many privileges and blessings.

These were our beginnings. Following this pattern of self-reliance, fortitude and perserverance in spite of privation, personal loss and sorrow, the pioneers pushed ever on, exploring, charting the wilderness: Kentucky, Pennsylvania, Ohio, beyond the great Mississippi, over the Oregon Trail, always westward to the coast. Some lived to see their hopes and dreams come true. Others died long before their destination was reached, but they all had their part in the building of a great nation. This, we should never forget.

Selection

Heap high the farmer's wintry hoard!
    Heap high the golden corn!
No richer gift has Autumn poured
    From out her lavish horn.

    Let other lands exulting glean
        The apple from the pine,
    The orange from its glossy green,
        The cluster from the vine,

        But let the good old corn adorn
           The hills our fathers trod;
        Still let us, for His golden corn,
           Send up our thanks to God.

              John Greenleaf Whittier

'Twas the Week Before Thanksgiving

Adelaide Hechtlinger

Especially associated with childhood on the old farm was the keeping of the annual Thanksgiving. It was one of the days we reckoned by, the dividing line between summer and winter, as well as the days of reunions and festivities. The season's work, as far as the land was concerned, was expected to be done before Thanksgiving; and indoors, housecleaning with its vexations must be well out of the way.

The winter supply of applesauce must have been made ere this. The apples from the Mt. Warner orchard had been laid up, and a generous quantity of the juice had been boiled down to the consistency of thin molasses, with which to sweeten the sauce, for our forefathers were economical.

The old cider mill, which had been all the season screeching its protest against the use of one of Nature's best gifts by turning it into brandy, had uttered its last groan and stood with naked jaws and bending sweep, a ghastly spectacle, until another season should compel a renewal of its doleful cries. The apple-paring, with its array of tubs and baskets and knives and jolly faces before the bright kitchen fire, was completed, with the Halloween games of counting the apple seeds and throwing the paring over the head to see its transformation into the initials of some fair maiden.

The great day for the conversion of the apples into sauce had lately come and gone, for it must be delayed as long as possible, that it may not ferment and spoil. The stout crane that swung over the huge fireplace was loaded with one or more brass kettles filled with apples, sweet and sour in proper proportion, the

former being put at the bottom because they required more time to cook. Sprinkled through the mass were a few quinces if they were to be had, to give flavor, while over the whole was poured the pungent apple molasses which supplied the sweetening. The great danger was that the sauce should burn; and to prevent this, some housewives had clean straw prepared and laid at the bottom of the kettles, lest the apples should come in too near contact with the fire. It was an all-day process, but when completed, an article was produced which was always in order for the table, and which, if slightly frozen, was enjoyed with a keener relish than the ice-cream of the restaurants of today.

Monday was devoted, of course, to the weekly washing, and nothing must interfere with that.

Tuesday was the great day for the making of pies, of which there were from thirty to fifty baked in the great oven that crackled and roared right merrily in anticipation of the rich medley that was being made ready for its capacious maw. Two kinds of apple pies, two of pumpkin, rice, and cranberry made out the standard list, to which additions were sometimes made. Then, in our younger days, we children each had a patty of his own. These were made in tins of various shapes, of which we had our choice, as well of the material of which our respective pies should be composed. The provident among us would put these aside until the good things were not quite so abundant.

Was not that a breath equal to the "spicy breezes of Ceylon" that greeted us as the mouth of the oven was taken down, and the savor of its rich compounds penetrated every crevice of the old kitchen, like sacrificial incense? Then, as the pies were taken out and landed on the brick hearth, and a number of pairs of eyes were watching the proceeding with the keenest interest, it would not be strange if pies and eyes sometimes got mixed up. I remember once quite a sensation was produced in the little crowd because brother T. lost his balance, and, for want of a chair to break his fall, sat down on one of the smoking hot pies!

After cooling and sorting, the precious delicacies were put away into the large closets in the front entry or hall, which the foot of the small boy was not permitted to profane.

Wednesday was devoted to chicken pies and raised cake. The making of the latter was a critical operation. If I mistake not, it was begun on Monday. I believe the conditions must be quite exact to have the yeast perform its work perfectly in the rich conglomerated mass. In due time the cake is finished. The chicken pies are kept in the oven, so as to have them still hot for supper. The two turkeys have been made ready for the spit, the kitchen cleared of every vestige of the great carnival that has reigned for the last two days, and there is a profound pause of an hour or two before the scene opens.

The happy meetings, the loaded tables, the hilarity and good cheer that prevailed, checked but not subdued in after years as one and another of the seats are made vacant by their departure to the better land—these are things to be imagined, but cannot be described. Warner, in his 'Being a Boy,' says that the hilarity of the day is interfered with by going to meeting and wearing Sunday clothes; but our parents managed that wisely by dividing the day, the first half of it being kept religiously, but the afternoon being given up to festivity—by no means, however, common weekday work. This was wise, I say, because it would be almost cruel to allow a lot of young people to indulge themselves to the very extent of prudence, to say the least, in eating, and then sit down to reading good books. This distinction between relaxation and toil for pelf is, I think, too often forgotten nowadays, founded as it is on both religion and philosophy. I remember well the sad look mother gave my brother and myself after our having spent the afternoon in making a hen-house, a very 'cute operation, we thought, but which found no favor in her eyes, as contrary to the traditions of the forefathers.

But the day after Thanksgiving, it must be admitted, had its peculiar pleasures. I doubt if there was any other of the holidays of the year when we boys felt so strongly the sense of freedom, and it was all the sweeter because it was the last we should have before we were set to our winter tasks. Skating was pretty sure to be one of the sports, if the weather had been cold enough to make the ice strong; and indoors there remained for our keen appetite the broken bits of pie and cake, to say nothing of the remnants of turkey and fowl of the day before, and which were enjoyed with a keener relish, if possible, than at first.

I forgot in its more appropriate place to speak of the roasting of the turkey. This was done in a tin oven with an iron rod running through it, and also through the meat that was to be cooked. This was the spit. The meat was fastened to the spit with skewers, so that, by means of a small crank at the end, it could be made to revolve in order to cook evenly. The oven was in shape something like a half cylinder, with the open side to face the fire. but there was a still more primitive way of roasting a turkey, and one which was resorted to sometimes when our family was the largest. Room was made at one end of the fireplace, and the turkey was suspended by the legs from the

ceiling, where was a contrivance to keep the string turning, and of course with it the turkey. On the hearth was a dish to catch the drippings, and with them the meat was occasionally basted. The thing is accomplished much more easily now, but at an expense, I imagine, in the quality of the work.

It is interesting to observe the universality of some of the customs that were in vogue fifty and one hundred years ago. In looking over the Centennial of the Churches of Connecticut, I came across the remark that the festive board, so crowded with good things on Thursday, gradually took on a plainer and less profuse array of dishes, until it ended off on Saturday evening with a simple bowl of hasty pudding and milk. This was in Revolutionary times; but fifty years later, when I was a boy, the same practices prevailed; in fact, hasty pudding and milk was the standing dish for Saturday evening, as boiled Indian pudding was for Sunday's dinner. I have been reminded since reading this item of a couplet my brother once repeated to me when we were boys:

'For we know Northampton's rule to be
Fried hasty pudding 'long wi' tea.'

Expressive, if not elegant, and it shows Northampton, bating the slight innovation of the tea, was true to New England tradition.

The Christmas holidays, as they are now observed, were not known in the country towns then. New Year's presents were often made, and the "Happy New Year" greeting was passed when neighbors met each other; but with most people we were too near the Puritan age to hear the "Merry Christmas" so common today, without a shock as though it were a profanation.

Squanto

(?) - 1622

In his mind Squanto pictured the homecoming ahead of him. With the swift, light tread of an Indian, he hurried along the familiar trail. He had been away from his village "many moons," the Indians' phrase for the passing of time. It had been several of the white man's years since he had seen the faces of his family. It seemed like an eternity since he had sat with his friends before a fire in the village of the Pawtuxet Indians on Cape Cod where he had grown up. His feet could not carry him fast enough to this reunion he had so often dreamed about.

Squanto's heart beat faster as the landmarks became more familiar. At last he topped a rise in the land and drew in his breath before looking down upon his village. He was momentarily stunned. He could not believe what he saw. His village was deserted.

The lone Indian in the English clothes and hard shoes dropped to his knees. Surprise gave way to anguish. The long months of yearning had been in vain. His people had vanished.

After a long time, Squanto got to his feet. With a great sadness inside of him, he walked down through what had been a busy, thriving village. Everything was gone. The houses were empty. Grass grew tall along the paths. A few bones lay scattered about, bleached white by the sun. No one had lived here for a long time. Squanto had nowhere to go. Alone in the world, he made camp near his old home.

In the silence of the deserted village, Squanto was surprised one day when he heard footsteps approaching.

"I am Samoset," said the young brave standing before him.

"I am Squanto of the Pawtuxets. Can you tell me where my people have gone?" he asked, relieved to have someone to talk to.

"A long time ago, a great sickness came," was the reply. "Everyone died." Squanto slowly took in the meaning of this. "You are the only surviving member of the Pawtuxet tribe," Samoset went on. "Come. I will take you to my chief, the great Massasoit."

On the way to the village of the Wampanoags, Squanto told Samoset his story; how one day as a lad he had seen the white man's "great canoe with wings" anchored near his village. He had gathered up his furs to trade them for the white man's goods.

he and Samoset became good friends.

One spring day in March of 1621, Samoset made a startling discovery. He begged Squanto to go with him to see what was happening.

"The white men have come. They bring women and children. They build homes. Come and see for yourself. They call themselves Pilgrims."

What Samoset reported was true. On the land where Squanto had roamed as a boy, white men were busy building houses. Anchored offshore was one of their giant canoes. Introduced to the Pilgrims by Samoset, Squanto told them, I will be your friend. I know what it is like to be in a strange land far from home."

Squanto took his promise seriously and became the special friend of the Pilgrims. He moved to their village and taught them how to plant corn "in the spring when the oak leaves are no bigger than a mouse's ear," three or four grains of corn to a hill with a fish buried beneath them. The Pilgrims had no fishhooks, so he showed them how to weave nets and where to use them. He showed them which fruits and berries were good to eat, and where to find edible green plants. When the Pilgrims' food supplies ran low, Squanto conducted them on expeditions to the various Indian villages and acted as their interpreter in trading for food. He accompanied Edward Winslow to see Massasoit and interpreted for him in drawing up the Treaty of Plymouth.

On one occasion Squanto was held captive by a hostile tribe. When they threatened his life, he held them off with tales of the Pilgrims with their "thunder sticks," coming to avenge his death. Fear of the guns caused them to delay. A rescue party, headed by Miles Standish, arrived in time.

In November, 1622, Squanto was acting as guide and interpreter on an expedition around Cape Cod. One evening he fell ill with a fever. His companions did everything they could to make him comfortable, but within a few days, Squanto died. In his last hours, he asked Governor Bradford to pray for him that he might go to the English God in heaven. He bequeathed his personal belongings to his Pilgrim friends as remembrances of his love.

All the Pilgrims mourned his death. He had been a true friend, and they were well aware that without his help they might not have survived in this strange new land. His death was a great loss to them.

Squanto had approached in friendliness, but was unexpectedly and rudely seized. With hands and feet bound, he was forced into the dark hold of the great ship, along with other young braves from villages along the coast. The ship sailed to Spain, where the young men were put on the auction block and sold as slaves.

Squanto would never forget the Spanish monks who sympathized with their plight and helped them escape. Squanto made his way to England, where he found a home with a wealthy merchant.

Squanto told Samoset, "Mr. Slany was a very kind man, but he noticed my sad face, and knew of my longing to return home. So one day he told me, 'Now you will return to your homeland.' " Squanto, with a grateful heart, had parted with the man who had befriended him in a strange land. He had sailed on a ship that was coming to trade with the Indians along the New England coast. Being anxious to see his family and friends, he had left the ship early and finished the journey on foot.

Chief Massasoit welcomed Squanto and invited him to make his home with the Wampanoags. The villagers welcomed him into their midst, and

Julia F. Lieser

From *Famous American Indians and Tribes*, Copyright © 1977 by The Saturday Evening Post Company, Indianapolis, Indiana. Reprinted by permission of the publisher.

Autumn

Blythe Gwyn Sears

Autumn, you're a sun-bronzed fairy
　　With a golden wand,
Roaming through the sylvan byways
　　Like a vagabond,
Tinting summer's faded garments,
　　Tattered now and old,
Changing silvered maple foliage
　　Into burnished gold.

Fiery opals gleam in waters
　　As you saunter by;
Languid forests flush with beauty
　　When your steps draw nigh.
Amber marigolds and dahlias
　　Blossom where you stroll,
And ungarnered grain in cornfields
　　Gleams like Sutter's gold.

Purple grapes and ruby apples
　　Offer you their wine;
Russet nuts and pink persimmons
　　Bid you come and dine.
Asters robed in Tyrian satin
　　Bow with regal grace,
And, for you, the topaz spiders
　　Weave their silky lace.

Scattering your gold and copper
　　With a lavish hand,
And diffusing saffron vapors
　　Through the drowsy land,
You fill earth with subtle perfume,
　　Fairy vagabond,
And refurbish tarnished beauty
　　When you wave your wand.

The Two Leaves

Felix Salten

The leaves were falling from the great oak at the meadow's edge. They were falling from all the trees.

One branch of the oak reached high above the others and stretched far out over the meadow. Two leaves clung to its very tip.

"It isn't the way it used to be," said one leaf to the other.

"No," the other leaf answered. "So many of us have fallen off tonight, we're almost the only ones left on our branch."

"You never know who's going to go next," said the first leaf. "Even when it was warm and the sun shone, a storm or a cloudburst would come sometimes, and many leaves were torn off, though they were still young. You never know who's going to go next."

"The sun seldom shines now," sighed the second leaf, "and when it does it gives no warmth. We must have warmth again."

"Can it be true," said the first leaf, "can it really be true that others come to take our places when we're gone and after them still others, and more and more?"

"It is really true," whispered the second leaf. "We can't even begin to imagine it; it's beyond our powers."

"It makes me very sad," added the first leaf.

They were silent a while. Then the first leaf said quietly to herself, "Why must we fall . . . ?"

The second leaf asked, "What happens to us when we have fallen?"

"We sink down. . . ."

"What is under us?"

The first leaf answered, "I don't know, some say one thing, some another, but nobody knows."

The second leaf asked, "Do we feel anything, do we know anything about ourselves when we're down there?"

The first leaf answered, "Who knows? Not one of all those down there has ever come back to tell us about it."

They were silent again. Then the first leaf said tenderly to the other, "Don't worry so much about it, you're trembling."

"That's nothing," the second leaf answered, "I tremble at the least thing now. I don't feel so sure of my hold as I used to."

"Let's not talk any more about such things," said the first leaf.

The other replied, "No, we'll let be. But—what else shall we talk about?" She was silent and went on after a little while, "Which of us will go first?"

"There's still plenty of time to worry about that," the other leaf assured her. "Let's remember how beautiful it was, how wonderful, when the sun came out and shone so warmly that we thought we'd burst with life. Do you remember? And the morning dew, and the mild and splendid nights. . . ."

"Now the nights are dreadful," the second leaf complained, "and there is no end to them."

"We shouldn't complain," said the first leaf gently. "We've outlived many, many others."

"Have I changed much?" asked the second leaf shyly but determinedly.

"Not in the least," the first leaf assured her. "You only think so because I've gotten to be so yellow and ugly. But it's different in your case."

"You're fooling me," the second leaf said.

"No, really," the first leaf exclaimed eagerly, "believe me, you're as lovely as the day you were born. Here and there may be a little yellow spot, but it's hardly noticeable and only makes you handsomer, believe me."

"Thanks," whispered the second leaf, quite touched. "I don't believe you, not altogether, but I thank you because you're so kind; you've always been so kind to me. I'm just beginning to understand how kind you are."

"Hush," said the other leaf, and kept silent herself for she was too troubled to talk any more.

Then they were both silent. Hours passed.

A moist wind blew, cold and hostile, through the tree tops.

"Ah, now," said the second leaf, "I . . ." Then her voice broke off. She was torn from her place and spun down.

Winter had come.

A Time for Thanksgiving

The harvest has been gathered
From orchards and the fields;
And mankind shares the bounty
That Mother Nature yields.

The hayloft holds a fragrance,
And granaries are replete
With sacks of oats and barley,
And piles of golden wheat.

The cellar bins are bulging
With apples, gold and red.
Squash and pumpkins occupy
The spaces overhead.

In cupboards by the stairway,
On sturdy shelves, will stand
The jars of fruit and jellies
That thrifty housewives canned.

Let windstorms howl in fury
And let cold winter strike!
This is Thanksgiving season
For man and beast alike.

Reginald Holmes

Common Market

How colorful the marketplace
When summer crops are in,
The ears of corn with yellow teeth,
Zucchini long and thin.

Asparagus with tufted heads,
The eggplant's purple sheen,
And artichokes with tender hearts
As served in haute cuisine.

The bursting bins of honeydew
And grapes of muscatel
Vie with apples gold and red,
While peaches blush and sell.

And all across this land of bliss
Thanksgiving is a time
To count the blessings from the hand
Of Him who is sublime.

Jayne Giammarino

Thanksgiving

Dale Matheson

Ah, time of magic, painted days
When harvest ends and fancy plays
Mid maple trees all turned to gold
By kiss of first October cold!

Bright bushes burn upon the ground;
Above, wild geese honk southward bound;
Frosts paint woodlands every shade
Of red and orange God has made.

Ripe pumpkins lie in golden mounds
Where turkeys feed with cozy sounds,
And, through the mellow purple haze
Enchanting all these autumn days,
Indians are seen to dance again
Around sumac fires in the glen
Where corn shocks rustle row on row
Like teepees in the long ago.

The fall of leaves or birds in flight
Seem arrows darting through the light;
Down russet highways of the year
The throb of tom-toms comes quite clear.

By night a round red moon rides high,
A pirate's doubloon in the sky.

And in these smoky dream-filled days
Thanksgiving draws a nation's praise
For fruitful fields and winnowed land,
All largess from a kind God's hand.

A Touch of Autumn

Sigurd F. Olson

Autumn comes without warning at a time when the lush, fruitful days of midsummer are beginning to wane, but when it still seems as though food, endless plenty, and warmth must go on forever. It may announce itself with just a touch of coolness on some bright morning toward the end of August, or by a few high leaves barely tinted with color, perhaps a spot of rusty gold on the bracken, or a tuft of grass turning sere.

All young are grown now, ready to leave nests, spawning beds, dens, and shelters. Then, almost imperceptibly, a burst of activity is evident in a growing urge to store food, in a scrambling for seeds, cones, and dried fungi, and in the mounting piles of birch and aspen branches around beaver houses. New birds appear, gathering for the migration south, and there is excitement in the air, with strange wings at dusk over marshes and lakes and in the sense of little time and that all must hurry before it is too late.

Woven through all this is the dramatic phenomenon of color—at first hints and flecks of it floating in the gloom of the woods, then the bright and pastel shades of shrubs beneath the trees, and at last the trees themselves in such flaming magnificence it is almost more than can be borne. The north becomes a land of blue and gold, and skies once more are alive with the movement of myriad birds.

At last all the flamboyant beauty is on the ground, on portages and in pools and along lake shores. A somberness comes to the land and with it a feeling of welcome quiet and relief to all living creatures who stay on.

Autumn

Henry Wadsworth Longfellow

With what glory comes and goes the year!
The buds of spring, those beautiful harbingers
Of sunny skies and cloudless times, enjoy
Life's newness, and earth's garniture spread out;
And when the silver habit of the clouds
Comes down upon the autumn sun and with
A sober gladness the old year takes up
His bright inheritance of golden fruits,
A pomp and pageant fill the splendid scene.

There is a beautiful spirit breathing now
Its mellow richness on the clustered trees,
And, from a beaker full of richest dyes,
Pouring new glory on the autumn woods,
And dipping in warm light the pillared clouds.
Morn on the mountain, like a summer bird,
Lifts up her purple wing, and in the vales
The gentle wind, a sweet and passionate wooer,
Kisses the blushing leaf, and stirs up life
Within the solemn woods of ash deep-crimsoned,
And silver beech and maple yellow-leaved,
Where autumn, like a faint old man, sits down
By the wayside a-weary. Through the trees
The golden robin moves. The purple finch,
That on wild cherry and red cedar feeds,
A winter bird, comes with its plaintive whistle
And pecks by the witch-hazel, whilst aloud,
From cottage roofs the warbling bluebird sings,
And merrily, with oft-repeated stroke,
Sounds from the threshing-floor the busy flail.

Oh, what a glory doth this world put on
For him who, with a fervent heart, goes forth
Under the bright and glorious sky, and looks
On duties well performed, and days well spent!
For him the wind, ay, and the yellow leaves,
Shall have a voice, and give him eloquent teachings;
He shall so hear the solemn hymn, that Death
Has lifted up for all, that he shall go
To his long resting-place without a tear.

Fall Approaching

There's a different feeling in the air these days; the mornings are crisp and the nights nippy. The trees in the yard are preparing for a change. Leaves on the maples are tinged with yellow. Red is beginning to show on the dogwoods, reminding us of the scarlet beauty they will soon wear. The craggy old walnut tree outside my window is beginning to release its foliage to the wind, and swirls of leaves fly over the fence into the garden or ride high over the hill toward the far horizon. Some cling to the ground to make a carpet for children and kittens and puppies to play on. The little stream flowing through the pasture carries leaf boats down to the water gate. There they will pile up until a hard rain swells the stream and washes them up on the bank where they will be left to dry or be blown away in a colorful cloud. A sudden hard shower whips the green-clad nuts off the old walnut tree. They thunder onto the roof, bounce down to the ground, and burst open, revealing the shiny black shells which contain crunchy, delicious meat. I must hurry to gather up these tasty morsels or my aging squirrel friend will snatch them away and bury them in his secret winter pantry. The geese that live in our area seem restless now. They fly their V formations between ponds often and noisily. Will they leave us this coming winter? Tabby and her kittens lie around in the sun, soaking up warmth they will need a little later. Tippy looks for a sheltered place to take his naps, rising up only long enough to greet his master or to bark, long and loud, at any stranger who may appear. He doesn't worry about the chilly days ahead. He has a snug little house and a fond mistress who caters to his every wish. The last hay has been cut and the aroma entices the cows from their favorite cud-chewing spot near the brook to the pasture gate. But they must wait until snow flies to get a taste of this delicacy.

Goldenrod, which has brightened the roadsides and hilltops all summer, is beginning to lose its yellow glow, but sturdy stems support the blossoms against wind and rain. Now, they wait for frost to paint them a shimmering white. The cider mill has been set up in the orchard and everyone must lend a hand to pick up the red apples which cover the ground. All must take turns washing and grinding the colorful heaps into sweet cider which will be stored in the cellar. Grape vines which, a few weeks ago, hid bunches of purple gems in deep foliage now cling to a few brown leaves as though to hold the warm days a while longer. Orange-colored pumpkins make huge polka dots in the cornfield, waiting for eager children to pick their jack-o-lanterns. All growing things are preparing for a long rest, and we must bid a fond farewell to summer. Now, we look forward, with grateful hearts, to Thanksgiving time and the short, quiet days of winter, with its snowy white blanket covering the ground.   Agnes M. Bell

According to an old legend, they came to grow on Cape Cod, Massachusetts, through the intervention of a white dove. During an argument, probably over whose "medicine" was the most powerful, an Indian medicine man cast a spell and mired the Reverend Richard Bourne in quicksand. In order to settle their differences, the two men agreed to a fifteen-day marathon battle of wits. Unable to move in the quicksand, the Reverend Bourne was kept alive by a white dove, which fed him a succulent berry from time to time. The medicine man could not cast a spell on the dove, and finally fell to the ground, exhausted from his own lack of food and water. The spell on the Reverend Bourne was released. In the course of these events, one of those little berries fell upon the ground and took root.

What was that bright red berry? Why, the cranberry, of course. And thus begins the history of one of North America's favorite native fruits.

The eastern Indians knew cranberries as "Sassamanesh." The Cape Cod Wampanoag and the South Jersey Leni-Lenape tribes called the little red berry "Ibimi," or bitter berry. The Algonquians of Wisconsin called them "Atoqua." And among the Delawares in New Jersey, cranberries were the symbol of peace. The Delaware chief Pakimintzen distributed cranberries at tribal peace feasts, and thus his name came to mean "cranberry eater."

The Indians had many uses for the cranberries they found growing wild in the lowlands. One dish they relished was pemmican, a mixture of dried venison, fat and cranberries, pounded to a pulp, patted into cakes and placed on rocks to bake in the sun. (Pemmican is often used today by hikers, with cranberries a vital ingredient.) A cranberry poultice was a remedy commonly used for treating wounds inflicted by poisoned arrows. The juice of the cranberry added brilliant color to the Indians' rugs and blankets.

With the landing of white people on this continent, the Indians discovered yet another use for their berry. As a sign of friendship, they presented the Pilgrims with gifts of cranberries. In fact, it is believed that cranberries were present at the first Thanksgiving feast in 1621.

With their introduction to this tasty fruit, the Pilgrim women applied their own culinary know-how in developing sweetened preserves, tarts and cranberry sauces. As early as 1683, a recipe for cranberry juice was published in *The Complete Cook's Guide*:

Put a teacupful of cranberries into a cup of water and mash them. In the meantime, boil two quarts and a pint of water with one large spoonful of oatmeal and a very large bit of lemon peel. Then add the cranberries and as much fine Lisbon sugar as shall leave a smart.

Wild cranberries remained popular as the Pilgrim settlements became thriving towns. Each fall, entire families gathered to pick enough to preserve for winter. In 1773, one Cape Cod community decreed a dollar fine for anyone caught picking more than a quart of cranberries before the twentieth of September. In addition to losing a dollar, no small amount in those days, anyone who jumped the gun also lost all his cranberries!

It was not long before American colonists began exporting the little red berry to Europe. In England during the eighteenth century, a bottle of the foreign fruit brought five shillings, nearly $1.25. In 1844, a barrel of cranberries, en route to an American visitor in Hamburg, Germany, was shipwrecked off the coast of Holland. The barrel floated to the island of Terschelling, where it was found by a beachcomber. Disappointed with the contents, he scattered them over the ground, taking the barrel only. Later, floods washed the cranberries into low areas where they took root and flourished. To this day, cranberries still grow on Terschelling, but refuse to grow anywhere else in Holland.

While Europeans were just discovering the tastiness of the cranberry, colonial shipping merchants were becoming aware of the berry's other rare and essential qualities. During the heyday of clipper ships and long whaling voyages, American ships carried cranberries in their holds to be eaten by sailors to ward off scurvy, much as English "limeys" ate limes. They had discovered that cranberries not

continued

only contained important vitamin C, but their natural waxy coating aided preservation over long periods of time.

With the prospect of economic gain from volume production of cranberries, experiments in cultivation began in Cape Cod, Massachusetts, about 200 years after the landing of the Pilgrims. At that time, Henry Hall of Dennis observed that cranberries seemed to grow larger and juicier where sand from the dunes blew over the vines. From his early observations in 1816, came other theories that started cranberries on their way to becoming an important business enterprise. As this business grew larger, cranberry cultivation spread—to New Jersey in 1835, Wisconsin in 1853, Washington State in 1883, and Oregon in 1885. Today, these states, including Massachusetts, still comprise the chief cranberry-growing regions of the world.

How are cranberries cultivated? To begin with, cranberry plantations are built on bogs, or peat swamps, that are drained of all water before they are cleared, leveled, spread with a layer of sand, and the vine cuttings set in. Acid peat soil, sand and a supply of fresh water are the three main requirements in cranberry cultivation. A new plantation usually takes from three to five years to bear a crop. With care and vigilance against frost damage, however, cranberry vines will bear indefinitely. Some producing cranberry bogs are over 100 years old.

Cranberries blossom in late June or early July. Their small, pink flowers are responsible for the cranberry's modern name. To the Pilgrims these blossoms resembled the heads of cranes; hence, the term "crane berry," later contracted to "cranberry."

The bright red hue the bogs assume in the fall signals the beginning of the cranberry harvest, extending from Labor Day through the entire fall season. In the early days, the fruit was picked by hand and the whole town would turn out for the harvest. Then for more than a hundred years, the berries were combed from the vines with wooden hand scoops. As the harvesters, down on their knees, moved across the bogs in diagonal lines, they pushed their wooden scoops before them, rocking them gently so that the smooth, wooden fingers removed the berries without damaging either fruit or vines.

Today, the wooden-tined cranberry scoop, a victim of mechanical replacement, is found more often in antique shops or in use in homes as a magazine rack, than in the harvesting of cranberries. In a few areas, however, where mechanical pickers are not feasible, a skilled scooper can harvest an average one hundred pounds of cranberries an hour.

Since the Indians first discovered them centuries ago, cranberries have certainly come a long way. They are now available year round in juices, sauces, jellies, breads, pies, relishes and just by themselves, frozen, canned or fresh. But the best way to really appreciate their goodness is on a plate between a buttery sweet potato and a steaming slice of turkey. Now that is something to be thankful for!

Berries For Your Table

SPICED CRANBERRIES

A tart and refreshing new way to serve fresh cranberries. This is a crisp and spicy accompaniment for meat or poultry.

1 lb. fresh cranberries
2 c. sugar
1 c. water
5 whole cloves
2 whole allspice
2 3-inch cinnamon sticks

Wash berries, remove stems, drain. In a large saucepan, combine sugar and water and bring to a boil over medium heat. Stir constantly until sugar dissolves. Add cloves, allspice and cinnamon; reduce heat and simmer 5 minutes. Add cranberries and simmer, stirring only one or two times, until berries start to pop, about 3 minutes. Remove from heat and cool. Pour into a 1-quart jar and refrigerate, covered, for several days before serving. Keeps indefinitely.

CRANBERRY NUT BREAD

Nut breads are a happy holiday thought. They will taste even better and be easier to slice if they are tightly wrapped and set aside for a day.

2 c. flour
1 c. sugar
1½ t. baking powder
½ t. baking soda
1 t. salt
¾ c. orange juice
1 T. grated orange rind
1 egg, well beaten
¼ c. butter or margarine, melted
2 c. cranberries, coarsely chopped
 or halved
½ c. chopped nuts

Sift together flour, sugar, baking powder, soda and salt. Combine orange juice, rind, egg and melted butter. Add to dry ingredients and mix only until flour mixture is moistened. Carefully fold in cranberries and chopped nuts. Spoon into 2 greased loaf pans and bake in a 350° oven 1 hour.

CRANBERRY MOLD

A tradition at holiday dinners, here is one way to serve cranberries.

2 pkgs. cherry gelatin
2 c. boiling water
 Pineapple juice (plus water to make 1 c.)
1 lb. fresh cranberries
1 medium orange
1 c. sugar
1 7-oz. can crushed pineapple, drained
¼ c. chopped nuts (optional)

Dissolve gelatin in boiling water; add pineapple juice plus water. Stir and chill until of jelly-like consistency. Coarsely grind cranberries and orange. Drain and discard liquid. Add sugar and let stand for 10 minutes. Add crushed pineapple and nuts and stir into semiset gelatin. Spoon into lightly oiled 6-cup mold and refrigerate until firm. Serves 10 to 12.

CRANBERRY PUDDING

This very special recipe is unique to the Midwest and has become a tradition in many households at holiday time. It is simple to prepare.

1 egg, slightly beaten
1 heaping T. sugar
½ c. light molasses
⅓ c. hot water
1½ c. flour
2 t. baking soda
½ t. salt
2 c. fresh cranberries, washed and drained

Combine all ingredients in order listed. Pour into a greased mold and steam over simmering water, tightly covered, for 1 hour. Make a steamer by punching holes in an aluminum pie pan and inverting it in the bottom of a saucepan with a tight-fitting cover. Serve warm with the following sauce. No other sauce will do!

SAUCE

1 c. coffee cream
¼ lb. butter
1 c. sugar
¼ t. salt
1 t. vanilla

Mix together cream, butter, sugar and salt and heat to the boiling point. Remove from heat and add vanilla. Serve warm over warm pudding. Use the sauce liberally, as the pudding is tart.

A Voice Rang Out

Grace Noll Crowell

The frost came early those November nights,
The cornstalks withered, and the hills took fire
From the gold and scarlet of the autumn lights
That burned through painted leaves like fierce desire.

A partridge drummed,
A fox-bark rent the air,
The stockade gates were shut,
And none too soon,
The night in that strange region
Was a lair
For all wild things—
The golden harvest moon
Climbed slowly upward . . .
"We shall choose," they said,
"A special day
To render thanks to God."
So on the morrow
They had richly spread
Their tables with the good fruits
Of the sod.

"For these we offer thanks,"
A voice rang out,
A voice whose echo
Never has been spent.
Within the new land
It became a shout—
A settlement
Became a continent;
And men still offer thanks
And pause to pray
As the pilgrims did
That first Thanksgiving Day.

Thanksgiving — 1621

At harvest time in 1621
The Pilgrims viewed God's bounteous gifts at hand—
The woods and rivers rich with fish and game—
And felt an inborn kinship with this land.

The Indians, round about, had taught them much.
The Mayflower carried back their special claim,
An application for the right to hold
Good Plymouth as their home, in heaven's name.

Young William Bradford, governor now elect,
Remembered harvest days when he was young;
How joyous hearts would lift in prayer and praise,
How sumptuous feasts were spread and bells were rung.

Why not prepare a similar holiday
Before the snows of winter bound them in?
The Indians, too, would share the festival
And thankfulness would ring through hill and glen.

Messengers were sent to Massasoit,
Great chief and sachem of the tribes nearby,
Inviting him to come and bring his warriors.
Together they would thank the God on high.

Governor Bradford sent four men out fowling.
Some Pilgrims gathered shellfish on the shore.
Soon they returned with turkeys, eels and oysters.
Enough to feed them all a week or more.

When Massasoit arrived with ninety braves,
Faint hearts believed their winter foods were gone.
But this great chief remembered other harvests.
They, too had danced and sung in praise of corn.

Quickly, on command, he sent his hunters,
Those whose skill and cunning were the best.
Soon five fine deer, enough for ample servings,
Were given to the leaders and the rest.

Food was cooked and served out in the open.
Turkeys, deer and geese turned on the spits.
Lobsters and oysters roasted on the coals
While stews and chowders steamed and boiled a bit.

"Sallets" were served: parsnips, turnips, carrots,
Onions, cabbages, radishes and beets.
Biscuits and hoecakes browned; popcorn was popping.
Little "dough-case" berry pies were special treats.

Between the meals they joined in games of sport.
There were shooting expositions—bow and gun.
Captain Standish led his military drills
And fired the shiny cannon just for fun.

The celebration lasted three long days.
Strong friendship ties replaced distrust and fear.
The Pilgrims and the Indians both agreed
To share Thanksgiving once again next year.

Alice Leedy Mason

The First Thanksgiving
Jennie Augusta Brownscombe
American, 1850 - 1936

THANKSGIVING

Thanksgiving: a religious celebration seasoned with secular flavor; Pilgrims in their newly-adopted homeland giving thanks for divine goodness; brimming baskets of harvested bounty; love's labors admired; paying homage to the land and to the wonders of nature; folded, prayerful hands giving thanks for the blessings of the years; clouds brimming with snowflakes ready and waiting to fall; Indian corn swishing and fallen leaves swirling in the wind; travels to home sanctuaries; all the relatives relating; hearts touched and love renewed; a treasury of remembered blessings built on happy talk of happy times; the special aroma of Mom's kitchen that encourages us to lift lids; stretched out torsos and toasted toes; eyes attached to football games; drumsticks, stuffing, and traditional treats heaped on the table; home-canned goods opened for sharing; cranberry sauce, olives, and large pieces of pumpkin pie with scooped vanilla ice cream; hopeful wishing on the wishbone; a day for falling asleep in the easy chair; a day's ordinary business forgotten in the coincidences of celebration; being thankful for the best in the best of all possible worlds; a warm, cozy, comfortable condition of the body, mind, and spirit. Thanksgiving is a way of being.

Elaine C. Frantz

JOHN SLOBODNIK

Thanksgiving

Mary Borrelli

For the bounty of Your love, O Lord,
We offer thanks today,
As gathered round the festive board
We bow our heads to pray

For all of those who love us, Lord,
And all of those we love,
For the gracious harvest of Your gifts,
Your guidance from above.

For the things we take for granted
Throughout our busy year,
We pause to thank You, Father,
Today, in heartfelt prayer.

The Grace of Gratitude

J. Harold Gwynne, D.D.,

As we receive Thy bounties, Lord,
Of raiment, shelter, food,
Inspire within our minds and hearts
The grace of gratitude.

All gifts and blessings that we know
Come from Thy gracious hand;
Thy overruling love and power
Encompass sea and land.

The sun that shines, the rains that fall,
The soft blue sky above;
The winds that blow, the clouds that drift,
Are tokens of Thy love.

The orchards bearing ripened fruit,
The fields of golden grain,
The trees and flowers everywhere,
Thy mercies, Lord, contain.

Creator of these lives of ours,
With every gift endued,
May all our days and years express,
The grace of gratitude.

I'm Thankful

I'm thankful for a lot of things,
    I'm thankful, so I say;
I'm thankful for the big outdoors
    Where I can run and play.

I'm thankful for Thanksgiving Day—
    For pies all in a row.
I'm thankful Grandma made them sweet—
    She knows I like 'em so.

I'm thankful for the turkey, too,
    How brown it is, and nice!
And I'd be very thankful, please,
    For only one more slice!

Author Unknown

Family Reunion

The fireside is warm with a radiant glow
    That dances upon the wall,
And the savory scents from the kitchen range
    Are intriguing us one and all,
While we greet with joy and love in our hearts
    The relatives from miles away,
With a smile and a kiss, and a warm embrace
    At Grandmother's house today.

The table is laden with the holiday feast
    That draws our happy sighs,
With a meal that only Grandma can prepare
    To captivate our eyes;
Soft mashed potatoes are fluffy and white
    And the turkey is roasted brown,
While dressing and gravy and hot bread rolls
    Are waiting to be passed around.

The moment is near when Grandfather nods
    For us all to bow our heads
And humbly give thanks for this wonderful day
    And for this our daily bread . . .
"We come to Thee, God, with grateful hearts
    For Thy bountiful gifts from above,
And each day may we feel Thy guiding hand
    And the presence of Thy love."

Joy Belle Burgess

Thanksgiving Song

This is the day the Lord hath made;
Be glad, give thanks, rejoice;
Stand in His presence, unafraid,
In praise lift up your voice.
All perfect gifts are from above,
And all our blessings show
The amplitude of God's dear love
Which every heart may know.

The Lord will hear before we call,
And every need supply;
Good things are freely given to all
Who on His word rely.
We come today to bring Him praise,
Not for such gifts alone,
But for the higher, deeper ways
In which His love is shown.

For sin destroyed, for sorrow healed,
For health and peace restored;
For Life and Love by Truth revealed,
We thank and bless the Lord.
This is the day the Lord hath made,
In praise lift up your voice.
In shining robes of joy arrayed,
Be glad, give thanks, rejoice.

Laura Lee Randall

Simple Pleasures

The very simple pleasures
In this big world of ours
Will bring you truest happiness
And let you touch the stars.

They are all around you
As you go along your way:
Gold and pink dawn of the morning,
Crimson sun at close of day.

Nature's lovely wonders,
A tree, a blade of grass,
Flowers gaily blooming,
Songbirds when you pass,

Wood and field and hamlet,
Valley, hill and stream,
Quiet, peaceful places
Where you can rest and dream.

Ropes of golden sunshine,
Silver drops of rain,
Rainbows you can wish on,
And a shady country lane.

Laughter of the children,
Homes tucked side by side,
Cheerful, helpful neighbors,
A doorway open wide,

Smiles of your loved ones,
Memories held dear,
Spring and summer, autumn,
And winter when it's here.

Little deeds of kindness,
Asking no reward,
Yet weaving hope and faith
Into a strong and lasting cord.

A candle casting magic beams,
A quiet, holy prayer,
The knowledge in our hearts,
That God is always there.

The trust in one another,
A handclasp of a friend,
All these are simple pleasures
And can never really end.

For they are here for all of us
To enjoy each day we live.
Just look around and you will find
Sheer joy they always give.

How great the simple pleasures
Too numerous to count,
And if you stop to see them
They ever seem to mount.

LaVerne P. Larson

This Thanksgiving Day

Once more the nights have lengthened,
The air has colder grown.
The frost has nipped the woodland,
And the birds have southward flown.

Autumn's splendor has now faded
And the trees are bare and brown.
At every gust of chilly wind
We see leaves tumbling down.

Twirling, they scurry across the lawn;
Above, the bare tree grieves,
And there I see across the way
My neighbor raking leaves.

The flowers are dead and turned so sere,
. . .So sere in every garden row,
Except there by the old stone wall
The chrysanthemum's colors glow.

Time goes by so very fast;
Again we see it's fall,
And there in lines across the sky
We hear the wild geese call.

The golden corn is garnered;
There are apples in the bin,
And the barns with hay are bulging;
All the harvest gathered in.

Then we bow our heads in reverence,
Say a prayer of gratitude,
And give thanks for home and family,
And the good supply of food.

Then we think about the Pilgrims,
Those brave folks of long ago,
And about the first Thanksgiving
And New England's ice and snow.

Then the landscape seems to brighten
And we know our land is fair,
With its wealth of season's beauty
And the tangy autumn air.

Let us then give thanks sincerely,
And in reverent words to say,
Thank You, God, for all our blessings
And for this Thanksgiving Day.

R. Glenn Jones

More Fireplace Pleasure
Blanche Campbell

It's fireplace time. After all, there is no place more inviting on a cold, wintry night. As family and friends gather round, make it the center of attraction.

If you are building a new home, give a lot of care and thought to the planning of the fireplace. It is still a major feature of the living room (or family room). Tiny fireplaces look out of place in the spacious living quarters of a modern home.

Clay tile which is fireproof and can resist smoke damage is an excellent choice in materials. Extend the facing from the floor to the ceiling, or run it along an entire wall of the living room.

Locate the fireplace on an inside wall to maintain a better draft. It will save both labor and building materials. But before you choose a definite location, study the room with an eye towards furniture arrangement, too.

If possible, build a wood storage locker when you install the fireplace. If this can be arranged with a back door opening into a garage or outdoors, it will save carrying fuel into the room.

Woods to burn

Resinous woods, such as pine and hemlock, are unsuitable for a fireplace unless you want to keep a fire screen up all the time, shutting away the pleasure of an open fire. These woods sputter, explode, and send off flying sparks which can even become dangerous.

Oak and beech are the best woods for an open fire, with ash, birch and other hard woods making close seconds.

Elm will also give you satisfaction when mixed with other, better woods. But when burned alone it gives a dull, uninteresting fire.

There is a knack to fire building. For best results, place the thickest log in the back. And the thicker this log the better. In olden times this log was often thick enough to last a year.

In front of this thick log, pile other logs, then thrust the kindling under them. The small logs will burn in the middle and the pieces fall to the hearth. Use tongs to replace them if they fall outside the bars.

Allow the ashes to accumulate until they almost reach the lower side of the bars, then remove only part of them. Ashes hold heat and bank the fire, keeping it from going dead.

When starting a fresh fire or when the back log is burned through, use the poker to draw the burned log to the front, making way for a fresh large log at the back. This gives you a better fire. It's also more economical to have the large, slow-burning log at the back of the fire and the blazing ones in front.

For cozy driftwood flames, place a small piece of broken copper screen in the fireplace. This will produce a driftwood blaze that will last at least several months without renewing.

Removing ashes

Before attempting to remove ashes from the fireplace, first dampen with a light sprinkling of water. This acts as a safety precaution to put out any live coals. It also keeps the dust down, preventing it from flying about. Ashes should always be taken up in a steel coal hod or pail.

When fireplace screens become dingy, dull and old-looking, give them a good brushing with a wire steel brush to remove all loose dust and soil. Then give the screen a coat of black liquid shoe polish. After it dries thoroughly, buff with a shoe brush and your screen will have a shiny, new black finish. This is quick, easy and inexpensive.

Now you are ready to sit back and enjoy the cheeriness of your brightly-burning fire. It extends warmth to the body and cheer to the spirit.

I, November   Faith Baldwin

November leaves us her color. Perhaps you don't think she has color to give, but she has. After the bright leaves are gone, a few hardy ones remain, and the color of the oak leaves, a pink-brown, faded and lovely, is something I always welcome. For years, I've been looking for a tweed just like it.

There are jewels in November, too; the scarlet of the elderberries in the woods, for instance.

November has brought us Thanksgiving and a reminder that it isn't, really, just one day in a year, set aside by Presidential Proclamation. It's for every day. Of course turkey every day would be somewhat wearing, but the giving of thanks can be for any time and any hour—and should be.

I am grateful for so much, and each day for something more. Sometimes it's a negative gratitude, for when a day's been very difficult, I'm glad that it ends, but glad, too, that in all probability I'll open my eyes, after sleep, on a new one.

Nowadays it snows here more often in this month than it did in years past. I remember a Thanksgiving snowfall which the weatherman said was the first in forty years. I also remembered, forty years before that, being driven through city streets in a sleigh to my grandmother's for dinner.

The old order changeth, but sometimes it returns.

I am grateful for Thanksgivings past, for this one, and for those to come. I am grateful for collected memories and for the tide which takes me toward the source of all living.

The legacy of Thanksgiving is gratitude, the harvest is love.

And I have birthdays to recall in this month, which takes us into the Christmas season, and a wedding anniversary, my own.

So, thank you, November.

From *Harvest of Hope* by Faith Baldwin. Copyright © 1962 by Faith Baldwin Cuthrell. Reprinted by permission of Holt, Rinehart and Winston, Publishers.

Stella Craft Tremble

Nearly thirty years ago, the poetry of Stella Craft Tremble first appeared in *Ideals* magazine. Since then, over ten thousand of her poems have been published world wide. Upon graduation from Eastern Illinois Teachers College in 1922, Stella Tremble began her teaching career. In 1956, she started the first of three quarterly poetry magazines which still exist: *The Prairie Poet, The American Poet,* and *United Poets.* After serving two terms as president of the American Poetry League, Stella Tremble was made life-President of the American Poets Fellowship Society, a growing corporation with many poets. Among her many honors are several honorary doctoral degrees and awards for peace efforts through poetry. Her work, including inspirational articles, has appeared in numerous publications, including *The Upper Room* and *The Christian Science Monitor.* For sixteen years she shared stories with children in her local library in Charleston, Illinois, and wrote children's stories for *Story Art* Magazine. Stella Tremble continues to conduct poetry classes and seminars in the local high school. Several poetry books and anthologies are currently being added to her publication list.

The Frost Sprite

The frost with winter wand in hand
Puts coats of silver on the land,
Cuts etchings on the windowpane,
Puts beads of snow in autumn rain.

He paints the leaves with dainty brush,
And in the deepest woodland hush
He throws his silver everywhere
To dance with sunlight in the air.

Although Frost Sprite is full of pranks,
For all his fun we give him thanks.

The Cycle

Granaries are filled with corn in sheaves;
Down drift the brown and scarlet leaves.
The wren no longer sings the tune
He sang at lilac time in June.
Bushes are boasting snow-white plumes;
Cedars wear caps of glistening blooms. . . .
The sun tips southward, quite awry,
As wedges of wild geese honk by.
Bleak wintertime is near our land,
But to the ones who understand,
Whatever changes seasons bring,
The heart can have perpetual spring!

What Is Gold?

The pumpkins store their food in bags of gold
Near Indian corn heaped by in tawny shocks;
A wedge of wild geese feel the crispy cold
While honking through the azure skies in broken flocks.

The topaz plumes of goldenrod in fields
Where maples spill their coins along the fence
Nod at full apple trees that flaunt their yield;
A wood thrush sings a song in recompense.

Persimmons scent the frosty, tangy air,
And autumn's gold is sprinkled everywhere.

When Is Autumn?

When pearl-gray silver
Comes in the night
To decorate windows
In etchings of white;
When mornings are chill
And crispy with cold,
When nature is edged
With sapphire and gold;
When hills are clad
In mantles of red
And summer has taken
Her flowers and fled;
When silver haze wraps
Woods in a pall,
And birds are flying . . .
We know it is fall!

Thanksgiving Time

The Autumn season finishes the year,
Hangs harvest moon in cooler atmosphere.
Grain ripens, wheat and oats leap into shocks,
We hasten toward the year's last equinox . . .
For Winter hides behind a northern sky,
Floats in each wavering wind that flurries by.
Thanksgiving time, corn hurries toward the barn,
As ice forms isles on meadow-brook and tarn.
At borderland of every fertile field,
Marauding crows peck at remaining yield
Of grain dropped by machine or man, unseen . . .
They chatter as they sweep the furrows clean.
Apples, like small, red worlds, plunge down the night
On orchards, in mounds beautiful and bright.
Fall changes little as the years go by,
The prairie folk are glad . . . and so am I,
For every single blessing gives a reason
That we rejoice at this Thanksgiving season!

For Thy Blessings Great

We thank Thee, Thou God of harvest,
For ripened, golden grain,
For art of labor, heaven-blest,
For sunshine and for rain.

We thank Thee for the meadows wide,
For cattle, barns and hay,
For fertile plains and lovely woods,
For safety, night and day.

We thank Thee for the joy of life,
The fountain-spring of thought,
For glory of the setting sun,
For freedom, dearly bought.

And as the old year folds its wings
With song from wood and glen . . .
We thank Thee for Thy blessings great
And for Thy love,
Amen.

Sun Upon the Snow   Lansing Christman

There is reason to rejoice when a day or night of snow blankets the land. It seems as though the snow itself eases the chill, that it warms and comforts like a blanket on a bed. It shields the grass and grain; it softens and soothes.

A snow transforms the countryside into a world of elegance. There is dignity and tranquility in a woodlot. The snow has cloaked and draped the evergreens in caps and gowns of white. It is as though the softly falling flakes had stitched seams of white from needle to needle, from bough to bough, and from tree to tree. I think of pines stretching out their arms and holding hands in gestures of friendship and tenderness.

The tall white spires point to the sky from which the pure white gowns had come. The woodlot becomes a haven of content as one walks on under the bending boughs. And what purity unfolds across the hills when the sun comes to cast its brilliant light upon the snow-covered land!

Twilight Thanks   Myrtle Cook Jackson

November is the twilight of the year,
When autumn's sunset-glory fades from sight;
Soft shadows then like memories appear
To reassure our hearts before the night.
Across the harvest fields, all shorn and dry,
The frost has stitched a jeweled-silver trim;
The branches drape their lace against the sky—
All earth that fades, responds to autumn's whim.

This is the time when plenty breeds good will;
Now cordial gestures charm without dissent,
As hearth-fires chuckle loud to greet the chill
And hearts renew their joy and deep content.
We offer thanks for bounty's wide array—
Accept our hearts, O God, Thanksgiving Day.

Letter from Home

Gladys Taber

Now the days grow shorter, and nights have a tinge of frost.
In the evening we gather around the open hearth for popcorn and apples.

October is the drama of New England, the time of fulfillment after the hot summer and before the snow drifts deep in the valleys. The air smells of apples and wild grapes and woodsmoke. The trees in our valley blaze with garnet and gold and cinnamon-browns and the deep wine color of the oaks.

Days are crisp and nights meant for an apple-wood fire on the hearth, a bowl of shiny apples, and plenty of freshly popped corn dredged with butter and salt. At Stillmeadow the two small girls have moved into their fuzzy pajamas with feet (which are so hard to keep clean!). They have their bedtime snack by the fire. Kittens and dogs like to curl up and doze close to the hearth, and the rest of us just fit in around the edges.

Mankind's feeling for the open fire is basic, for in prehistoric times it was the discovery of fire that began man's climb from the jungles. Did lightning start his first one? Or was he rubbing stones together and a spark caught in some dead grass? Fire meant heat and protection from the great beasts, and meat that was cooked. And later some genius discovered that throwing grains and water in a pit of heated stones made a kind of mash that was edible. Charcoal grills and Cape Cod clambakes are present-day versions!

In our village we come together at the market, our social center, to discuss when the killing frost will arrive. Everyone is gathering the last garden crops—squash and beets and cabbages and late corn. Rows of jelly glasses glow on the pantry shelves. My favorite is elderberry, with its wine-dark color and tangy flavor—so good with roast lamb or pork.

The blessing of a dishwasher at this time cannot be overestimated. When I was growing up and my mother was doing her preserving and jelly-making, the range was full of big kettles boiling up jelly glasses and sterilizing pint and quart jars. It took more time to get the containers ready than to make the chutney or grape conserve or blackberry jam.

Now the dishwasher does the sterilizing all by itself. Sometimes I think we are snowed under by mechanical appliances in this era, but when I make a list of those I really love, next to the furnace (which runs itself) and the electric water heater I think I would put the dishwasher. I may go weeks without using mine, but then the children come and the kitchen is neck-deep in dishes, and it is a godsend.

The commercial jellies and relishes and preserves are delicious and infinite in variety. So all we need to do is to "put up a little of this and that," as we say, which makes us feel we are using nature's bounty. In our valley most women have a specialty, and at Christmastime gay jars and bottles are exchanged.

On Cape Cod now the cranberry harvest begins—still gathered in the long-tined scoops that are made of hard maple. The cranberry pickers go through the bogs on hands and knees, combing the berries out with the scoops. The Indians introduced the cranberries to the Pilgrims, but they were small bitter fruits and not the plump spicy jewels of today. Incidentally, one of the best relishes is cranberry relish.

Also on Cape Cod the scallop season begins, and this is the most delicate and savory gift of the sea. Scallops should be broiled very briefly with a bit of lemon juice and melted butter and dashes of paprika and salt.

When the geese go over, the long wedge of their flight arrows the sky with mystery. Do they realize how long the flight will be? How do they decide exactly when to start? Their cry is a lonely sound but breathtaking to hear. Perhaps one reason it is so moving is that it is a farewell to summer. I wish them well as I hear them go over, with a safe coming-back when it is time for them to return.

The next thing we know, the chickadees will be tip-tilting around and chatting away. It is time to clean the bird feeders and get the birdseed in and the cracked corn for the grouse and pheasants. Last winter my son-in-law put out a salt lick, and it was enjoyed; although we never saw the deer, we did see the tracks that these visitors had left in the snow.

At the moment there are berries and seeds and a few bugs and spiders, and plenty of nuts for the squirrels. There is time to walk to the pond and see the Hunter's Moon rise and hear the small owl in the apple orchard talking to the night. And time to dream of a world at peace, when the beauty of such a night might fill all hearts.

Daylight saving is over at the end of the month, but as I struggle with the clocks I realize man cannot control time. The sun rises when it is ready to rise and sets when it reaches the time to set. The moon keeps its appointed rounds no matter what our clocks say. I find it reassuring that we cannot yet regulate nature. Nature has a steadiness no nation has yet achieved. And as the seasons come and go, we know it is still a good earth that we live on. May we never destroy its wonder!

America the Beautiful

Katharine Lee Bates

O beautiful for spacious skies,
For amber waves of grain,
For purple mountain majesties
Above the fruited plain!
America! America!
God shed His grace on thee,
And crown thy good with brotherhood
From sea to shining sea!

O beautiful for pilgrim feet,
Whose stern, impassioned stress
A thoroughfare for freedom beat
Across the wilderness!
America! America!
God mend thine every flaw,
Confirm thy soul in self-control
Thy liberty in law!

O beautiful for heroes proved
In liberating strife,
Who more than self their country loved,
And mercy more than life!
America! America!
May God thy gold refine,
Till all success be nobleness,
And every gain divine!

O beautiful for patriot dream
That sees beyond the years
Thine alabaster cities gleam
Undimmed by human tears!
America! America!
God shed His grace on thee,
And crown thy good with brotherhood
From sea to shining sea!

We have received several requests from our readers asking for back issues of Ideals. With that in mind, we have listed the back issues of Ideals which are currently available. We trust this will allow you the opportunity to complete your personal library or order as a gift for any occasion. Write: Ideals Publishing Corporation, Dept. 107, 11315 Watertown Plank Rd., Milwaukee, Wisconsin 53226. Include just $3.00 for each title ordered. Postage and mailing will be included in this price.

POPULAR FAVORITES

Friendship Ideals '79
Carefree Days Ideals '79
Homespum Ideals '79
Autumn Ideals '79

SPECIAL HOLIDAY ISSUES

Christmas Ideals '78
Easter Ideals '79
Mother's Day Ideals '79
Thanksgiving Ideals '79
Christmas Ideals '79

COLOR ART AND PHOTO CREDITS
(in order of appearance)

Front and back cover, Freelance Photographers Guild; inside front and back covers, Alpha Photo Associates; Autumn trail, H. Armstrong Roberts; Sentinel Rock, Yosemite Valley, Yosemite National Park, California, Josef Muench; "Hill Country" near Ontario, Wisconsin, Ken Dequaine; Furry companion, Robert Cushman Hayes; Autumn's yield, Fred Sieb; Dahlias, H. Armstrong Roberts; Vermont countryside, H. Armstrong Roberts; Stream near Wonalancet, New Hampshire, Fred Sieb; Rustic setting near Snowville, New Hampshire, Fred Sieb; Bountiful harvest, Alpha Photo Associates; Thanksgiving scenic, H. Armstrong Roberts; Backyard bounty, Freelance Photographers Guild; Fox, H. Armstrong Roberts; Roadside beauty near Chocorua, New Hampshire, Fred Sieb; Lakeside retreat, Fred Sieb; Cranberries, Ralph Luedtke; THE FIRST THANKSGIVING, Jennie Augusta Brownscombe, Three Lions, Inc.; SAYING GRACE, John Slobodnik; Autumn bouquet, Colour Library International; Reverent moment, Fred Sieb; A COUNTRY ROAD, AUTUMN, William James Muller, Three Lions, Inc., Chapel near Aspen, Colorado, Ed Cooper; Sunrise flight, Canada geese, Appel Color Photography.

ACKNOWLEDGMENTS

MORE FIREPLACE PLEASURE by Blanche Campbell. Reprinted with permission from *Farm Wife News*, P. O. Box 643, Milwaukee, WI 53201. THANKSGIVING DAY by R. Glenn Jones. Used through courtesy of Mrs. R. Glenn Jones. GOD'S CORNER (October is a delightful month . . .) by Gertrude M. Puelicher. From *Exclusively Yours*, October 31, 1977. THE FROST SPRITE and WHAT IS GOLD? by Stella Craft Tremble. From *Wind in the Reed*, previously published by Bruce Humphries, Inc. Used with permission of the author. CRANBERRY PUDDING; SPICED CRANBERRIES; CRANBERRY MOLD; CRANBERRY NUT BREAD. From *Gourmet on the Go* by Naomi Arbit and June Turner. Copyright © 1974 by Ideals Publishing Corporation. APPLE CRISP; APPLE STRUDEL; APPLE DESSERT CRUNCH; BAKED APPLE MERINGUES; DUTCH APPLE KUCHEN. From *Tempting Treasures* by Gertrude Wright. Copyright © 1978 by Ideals Publishing Corporation. IT'S THE BERRIES. Information for article supplied by Ocean Spray Cranberries, Inc., Plymouth, Massachusetts. Our sincere thanks to the following authors whose addresses we were unable to locate: Fanny Stearns Davis for FOR A CHILD; Ella Castle Nedrow for AN AUTUMN WOOD; Laura Lee Randall for THANKSGIVING SONG; Dr. W. J. Thompson for BLESSINGS OFTEN OVERLOOKED.